JOBS
IN MY LIFETIME

Written by
Rebecca Phillips-Bartlett

American adaptation copyright © 2026 by North Star Editions, Mendota Heights, MN55120. All rights reserved. No part of this book may be reproduced or utilized in any form or by any means without written permission from the publisher.

Jobs © 2024 BookLife Publishing
This edition is published by arrangement with BookLife Publishing

sales@northstareditions.com
888-417-0195

Library of Congress Control Number:
2025930419

ISBN
979-8-89359-325-9 (library bound)
979-8-89359-409-6 (paperback)
979-8-89359-381-5 (epub)
979-8-89359-355-6 (hosted ebook)

Printed in the United States of America
Mankato, MN
092025

Written by:
Rebecca Phillips-Bartlett

Edited by:
Alex Hall

Designed by:
Jasmine Pointer

All facts, statistics, web addresses and URLs in this book were verified as valid and accurate at time of writing. No responsibility for any changes to external websites or references can be accepted by either the author or publisher.

Image Credits

Images courtesy of Shutterstock.com, unless otherwise stated.

Cover – EkaterinaKu, mhatzapa, Mar.stos, Andrew Rybalko. Throughout – Andrew Rybalko. 6–7 – NASA, Public domain, via Wikimedia Commons. 8–9 – Jack Weir (1928-2005), Public domain, via Wikimedia Commons, Freud, Andrew Bone from Weymouth, England, CC BY 2.0 <https://creativecommons.org/licenses/by/2.0>, via Wikimedia Commons. 10–11 – Jon Chica, Brzostowska. 12–13 – Everett Collection, Cineberg, balabolka. 14–15 – Antlii, Employee(s) of MGM, Public domain, via Wikimedia Commons. 16–17 – shironosov (iStockphoto) - seraficus (iStockphoto). 18–19 – Frame Stock Footage, Gorodenkoff, Everett Collection, Yuganov Konstantin, PeopleImages.com – Yuri A. 22–23 – Sri Rohayati, Nadya_Art.

CONTENTS

Page 4 Back in My Day
Page 6 When I Was Born
Page 8 When I Was Young
Page 12 I Remember...
Page 16 How Very Modern!
Page 18 Nowadays...
Page 20 Nana's Timeline
Page 22 Tomorrow's World
Page 24 Glossary and Index

Words that look like <u>this</u> can be found in the glossary on page 24.

BACK IN MY DAY

Layla was hard at work on her "What I Want to Be When I Grow Up" project. Her brother, Caleb, had lots of great ideas.

Jobs change as new things are <u>invented</u>.

Nowadays, computers can do math and solve problems for us. Before computers were as common, most math was done by people called human computers.

7

WHEN I WAS YOUNG

"What was your first job?"

"I got my first job when I was ten years old. I had a paper route!"

Every morning, Nana woke up very early before school. She rode her bike to the <u>newsstand</u> and picked up a stack of newspapers.

During high school, Nana had lots of part-time jobs. A part-time job is a job that someone only does for a few hours a week. This meant Nana still had time to focus on school.

"I worked in a store for a few years."

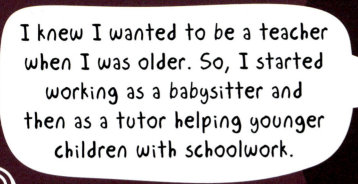

I REMEMBER...

"In 1982, Gramps and I got married. By then, I was working as a teacher and Gramps was a journalist."

A journalist is a person who writes news stories in newspapers and magazines. Journalists often race to be the first person to write a story.

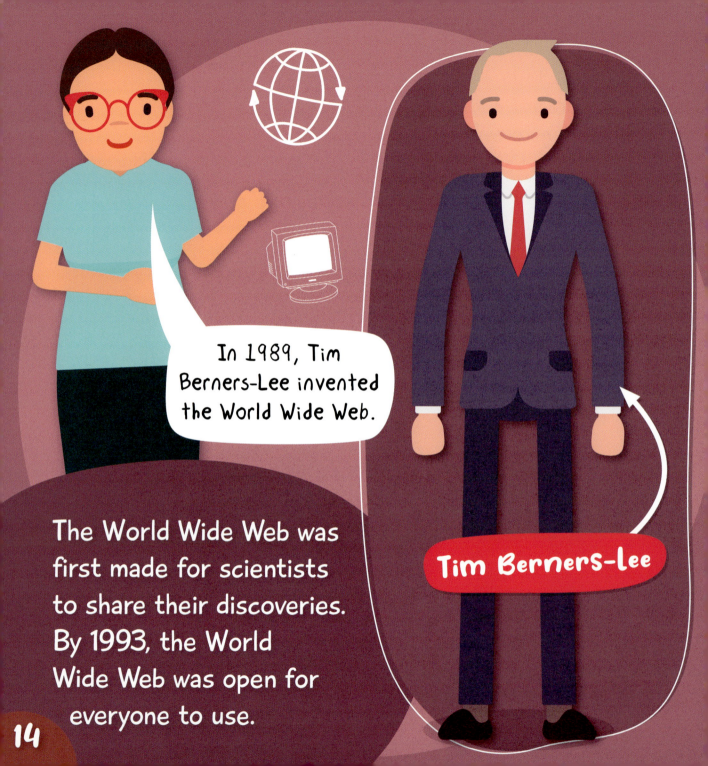

HOW VERY MODERN!

"By 2004, your mom was training to be a doctor. She used the internet and Wi-Fi a lot while she studied."

"Modern technology is still changing the world of medicine very quickly. New treatments are being discovered all the time."

Many doctors work to find new ways to keep people healthy. In the 1990s, new <u>vaccines</u> were invented.

Part of my job as a doctor is to give people vaccines.

Vaccines can save thousands of lives.

17

NOWADAYS...

As technology changes, jobs change too. Nowadays, there are all sorts of jobs that did not exist before.

Some people make new websites and apps or teach people how to stay safe online.

Some people invent new machines and <u>devices</u>.

18

However, many jobs that have existed for a long time are still needed today.

Teachers are very important. They teach the people who will become the inventors and scientists of the future.

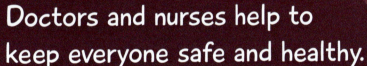

Doctors and nurses help to keep everyone safe and healthy.

NANA'S TIMELINE

"Jobs have changed a lot in my lifetime. Let's look back at my timeline."

1973–1981—Nana had part-time jobs working in a store, as a babysitter, and as a tutor.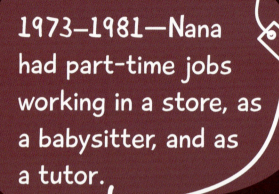

1969—Nana had a paper route.

1959—Nana was born. Her mom worked as a human computer.

1982—Nana and Gramps got married. Nana was a teacher. Gramps was a journalist.

1989—The World Wide Web was invented.

 1997—Wi-Fi was invented.

2004—Mom trained to become a doctor.

2009—Mom worked as a doctor and gave people vaccines.

TOMORROW'S WORLD

The world is changing quickly. Some jobs are not needed anymore, but there are lots of exciting opportunities for new jobs too.

GLOSSARY

devices	machines or inventions made to do something
interviewing	asking people questions to find out more about a topic
invented	when something new is created for the first time
modern	to do with recent or present times
newsstand	a shop or stand that sells newspapers and magazines
research	finding out more information to learn more about a topic
technology	inventions made using science
vaccine	medicine that is injected into a person or animal to protect against a disease

INDEX

computers 6–7, 20
doctors 16, 19, 21
internet 13, 16
journalists 12, 21

newspapers 8–9, 12–13
schools 8, 10
teachers 11–12, 19, 21